CHRISTIAN DAY SCHOOLS

CHRISTIAN DAY SCHOOLS
Why and How

by

D. L. KRANENDONK

Paideia Press
St. Catharines, Ontario, Canada

All Scripture quotations are from the Revised Standard
Version unless otherwise indicated.

Pictures and cover design by John Knight.

ISBN 0-88815-016-4

Printed in the United States of America.

This book is dedicated to the many parents and friends of Christian education who gave their time and often scarce financial resources to establish and maintain Christian day schools in North America.

Table of Contents

Part II
Reformed Christian Schools
and the International Union
of Christian Schools

Foreword

Christian education, much like Christian living, is capable of multiple expression. There is, and should be, Christian education going on in Christian homes, Christian schools, and Christian churches. Approaches may differ, emphases will vary, but the prime intent remains fixed. In the words of a 1642 document written to promote Christian learning on the North American continent: "Let every student be plainly instructed and earnestly pressed to consider well [that] the main end of his life and studies is to know God and Jesus Christ, which is eternal life (John 17:3), and therefore to lay Christ in the bottom as the only foundation of all sound knowledge and learning . . . . "

Sharing an awareness of the potential and blessing of Christian education is an ongoing task of all whose lives and communities have been blessed by it. Books, pamphlets, and other materials have been written to explain the basis and purpose of Christian day school operation, and we trust that more such publications will be written in the future. This book, *Christian Day Schools*, is the most recent of such works. It addresses current topics on the North American educational scene, analyzes basic issues, and puts forth Christian alternatives. Not every reader will agree fully with each presupposition or conclusion, but the message of the book is irrefutable: education that is true must be in keeping with the revelation of Him who said: "I am the Truth."

It is an honor for me to recommend this book to all who are seriously interested in struggling with the essentials of education today. An Old Testament admonition enjoins all to "get wisdom." The New Testament speaks of "Christ Jesus, who of God is made unto us wisdom." May this book be used widely to make that wisdom increasingly evident.

-Dr. Michael T. Ruiter
Executive Director
International Union of
Christian Schools
Grand Rapids, Michigan

Preface

North Americans believe that the quality of education is declining rapidly. That belief is supported by the sinking scores achieved by students taking college exams. Test scores are tumbling in spite of the billions of dollars spent annually to educate the young in both Canada and the United States. Costly studies have been conducted, theories proposed, and "innovations" tried. But concrete answers have not been found.

This book is an attempt to show that there is a Christian alternative view of life and the universe that can give us an understanding of the fundamental problems of education. Many Christian parents have already chosen the alternate system of education presented in this book.

The first part of this book raises some important fundamental questions about how Christians ought to relate to God, to each other, and to the world around them. The treatment of these questions is not academic or scholarly; neither is it exhaustive. The intention is merely to create a Scriptural reference map by which Christians will be able to reassess education as it relates to faith, the family, the church and the state.

The second part of this book will present a picture story of the Reformed Christian school, which will be followed by a look at many aspects of operating such a school. Finally we will take a brief look at the International Union of Christian Schools.

The basic theme throughout this book is that which can be found in the Bible, especially in John 1, Ephesians 1, Colossians 1, Hebrews 1, and other places. That theme is simply this: all things were created *in, through* and *for* God the Son, who was appointed by God the Father to redeem all things by destroying the defilement of sin. Even now Christ sustains the universe by His powerful command.

It is my hope and prayer that this book will help the reader gain a better understanding of and deeper insight into the beauty of education solidly founded on the Word of God. Readers who do not agree with the vision of life expressed in these pages should at least come to realize that *all education is at heart religious*, i.e. conducted on the foundation of faith in God, man, or something else.

I owe special thanks to Dr. Jack Fennema who, while he was Executive Director of the Ontario Alliance of Christian Schools (District 10 of the Union), raised questions and wrote papers which helped me focus more clearly on the issues of Christian education. I also would like to thank Dr. Sidney Kerr, C.V. (Chuck) Lawrence, Sidney Harkema, Irene Simpson, Mel Elzinga, Hans Vander Stoep, and Walter Piersma, all of whom served with me on the Public Relations Committee of the Ontario Alliance of Christian

Schools, where many of the ideas in this book were discussed and reviewed. My thanks also go to my dear friend Paul Davenport, with whom I had many hours of constructive conversation as this manuscript took shape.

Special recognition goes to the administrative staff of the union of Christian schools to which the vast majority of the schools based on the views expressed in this book belong. Dr. Michael T. Ruiter and his staff gave me constructive criticism and refreshing Christian support.

Finally I must mention my dear wife Henny, who not only gave me moral support but also served as my critic.

D. L. Kranendonk,
London, Ontario, Canada

Introduction
and
Historical Setting

North American education has arrived at a stage in its development where its internal problems and difficulties are causing upheavals and confrontations never witnessed before. In addition to a rapid decline in student performance, there is rising violence, taxpayer rebellion against high costs, teacher unrest, and apathy. A general feeling of frustration exists throughout the two major North American nations—a frustration with education that is especially evident in the larger urban centres.

North American educators seem to be polarizing into two opposing camps—those who want total freedom to educate

17

and live according to their own "free" conscience, and those who want a return to basic subjects and "law and order." Most orthodox Christians are champions and defenders of the "law and order" camp.

During the early history of the American "order," a sharp division between church and state developed. Church leaders and statesmen alike argued that the church and the state deal with two distinct and mutually exclusive areas of life. Both areas were initially recognized by Christian leaders as having their origin and source of authority in God. The state was given God's authority to govern "worldly" affairs, including education. The church received God's authority to govern the religious, "spiritual" aspect of life. There was one area where duplication of authority was thought to exist: the moral or value or norm side of all activities.

Although it was recognized that the state has authority in education, it was the organized church, both Protestant and Roman Catholic, that started most of the school systems in North America. There were a number of reasons why that early education was organized and operated by the church. First of all, the church had to educate children to read and write so that the younger generation would be able to carry on the mission of the church. Secondly, since the church was primarily a frontier church, it was usually the first and, for some time, the only organized institution in a new community. Thirdly, church and state both subscribed to the same Christian morals and values. Hence, since education was only perceived to be technical training in reading, writing and arithmetic, the state had no difficulty in letting the church cover these technical areas while teaching morals, values and "religion."

As North American society developed and became more complex, the doctrine of complete separation between church and state also took a pronounced turn. More and more, the organized church refrained from speaking out on the social and cultural aspects of life. In addition, orthodox Christians gradually stopped speaking about the meaning of the religious beliefs in the public and political areas of life.

The fact that Christians stopped expressing themselves on the meaning of their religious values and commitments in relation to life in general should not be seen as evidence of a decline in their faith in Jesus Christ as their personal Savior. With the increase in immigration from all parts of the world, the governments of the day, which were made up mostly of dedicated, churchgoing men, came to see that governments could not impose Christian religious views on all of the different religious groups in North America. It became apparent that imposing Christian religious views on society would amount to discrimination against Jews, Mormons, Mohammedans, and others. In this way a shift in emphasis developed in the original idea of separation between church and state. The idea gradually took root that the church was concerned with only religion, and that all other areas of life could be operated without religion or religious influences. The "worldly" areas of life had become neutral and secular.

Church leaders, then, revised their interpretation of the separation between church and state and shifted their emphasis somewhat. This soon had its affect on the development of day schools in North America. The state began to exercise its authority in secular education by taking over the establishment, operation, and funding of most school systems. In recent times the results of these gradual changes have become apparent to North American Christians. A militant atheism arose and gained much influence after World War II.

With the growth of atheism, pressure was placed on governments and public institutions to eliminate all references to and symbols of religion from the secular areas of life. One of the results was that Bible reading and prayer were removed from the public schools by order of the United States Supreme Court. The Court's landmark decision was taken as a logical conclusion of the modern interpretation of the constitutional principle of the separation of church and state. Bible reading and prayer in public schools is not in accordance with the constitutionally established "law and order," according to the Supreme Court justices. With that decision, man declared that there is no God in authority over man, and that man is his own master in all the secular areas of life. The claim that man is his own master is known as Humanism.

Although there was no supreme court decision in Canada, the same Humanist spirit prevails. In most Canadian public education systems, the Bible can only be used as a source book for comparative religion, or as a book of literature.

When the Bible, the authoritative Word of God, was removed from the public schools, the last symbol of an authority above man disappeared from the public educational arena. The problems which North American public schools now face — as do orthodox Christians who send their children to those schools — are a direct result of the removal of the Bible as God's authority. If children are taught in their school curriculum that the individual is his own master (god) in all the secular areas of life, then there can be no one who teaches the child what he should and must do in matters of conscience. According to the Humanist's concept of education, the child must be allowed to digest the objective facts presented to him in total freedom. Each child, it is argued, is basically good and has the inherent ability to create his own orderly universe out of the objective facts. The sovereignty of the child's personal conscience is considered to be absolute. Man has become his own god with full freedom to do what is right in his own eyes. The only legitimate restriction that the state may place on this "god-man" is to see to it that the actions of one individual do not deprive another individual of *his* right to be his own god.

The atheistic Humanist at first agreed that individuals had given some of their private rights to the state so that society could operate. By now, though, they argue that the individual can never surrender the freedom to live by the dictates of his autonomous conscience. They maintain that the only reason the state ever got involved in the area of morals and values was because of religious pressures by Christians.

Atheistic Humanism is a product of an education system that has rejected the fact that there is a sovereign God who rules all things. The atheistic Humanist wants all governments and government institutions to practice what is already being taught in the public schools. Atheistic Humanist man demands that governments stop imposing Judeo-Christian morals, values and norms on individuals. For him the state has no business legislating any statutes which assume a standard of right and wrong, for conceptions of right and wrong differ for each autonomous person. Concepts of right and wrong can differ from day to day, depending on the situation in which the "god-man" finds himself.

With such concepts of atheistic Humanism governing the public mind, it is not difficult to foresee anarchism as the ultimate, logical result of removing the authority of God from education. The result of the separation of church ("religion") and state ("secular") is coming home to roost. North American education cannot get out of this dilemma without first acknowledging the sovereignty of God.

Part I

The Relation between

God,

Man

and

Creation

1
The Word of God and Man

A prior question

At the center of every Christian's life lies the question: What does it mean to be a Christian? That question should not only be asked in times of crisis and frustration; it should be the basic question before starting any activity.

There is, of course, no one who claims to be a Christian and who, at the same time, does not have some concept of what that claim means to him or her. Some people claim to be Christians in the hope that if, by chance, there is an "afterlife," they will be part of it because of that claim. Others believe that being a Christian means total withdrawal from the world, as in monastic life, for example. Still others believe that being a Christian only has meaning for their spiritual life, that it has nothing to do with their daily affairs. As I noted earlier, that kind of view is widespread among North American Christians.

There is benefit in asking what it means to be a Christian only if one is willing to let the Word of God speak. All personal views and philosophies must be tested on the Word of God by means of the power of the Holy Spirit.

Who is man?

When we attempt to let the Word of God speak, we have no alternative but to turn to the Bible. There is no other means by which one can become aware of God's total plan and purpose than through the Bible.

The Bible tells the Christian that man is part of God's plan. God created all that is in heaven and on earth. God then created man* to look after, rule over, develop, and be accountable for all the earth and everything in it. In short, man is the servant of God.

> Then God said, "Let us make man in our image, after our likeness; and let them have dominion over the fish of the sea, and over the birds of the air, and over the cattle, and over all the earth, and over every creeping thing that creeps upon the earth." So God created man in his own image, in the image of God he created him; male and female he created them. And God blessed them, and God said to them, "Be fruitful and multiply, and fill the earth and subdue it; and have dominion over the fish of the sea and over the birds of the air and over every living thing that moves upon the earth." And God said, "Behold, I have given you every plant yielding seed which is upon the face

---

*Man as used in this book means both male and female (Gen. 1:27).

of all the earth, and every tree with seed in its fruit; you shall have them for food. And to every beast of the earth, and to every bird of the air, and to everything that creeps on the earth, everything that has the breath of life, I have given every green plant for food." And it was so. And God saw everything that he had made, and behold, it was very good. And there was evening and there was morning, a sixth day (Gen. 1:26-31).

From this reference it can be seen that man is *not* autonomous; he is *God's* man. That is true not only of the Christian but also of the non-Christian. The Christian serves God through the grace of salvation brought about by Jesus Christ through His perfect obedience. The non-Christian, who denies God's sovereignty and existence, cannot escape serving God; God even uses him to sustain His universe. Through the powerful command of the Creator and Redeemer, the non-Christian is forced to assist in the unfolding of God's plan whether he realizes it or not.

Who is God?

When man tries to understand or explain something in creation, it is absolutely necessary for him to be able to relate his ideas to something which he has previously experienced. A person can understand what is meant when someone yells, "Fire!" only because the word immediately calls up a previous experience to which that word relates. But go to the natives in the Amazon jungle and yell, "Explosion!", and you will get a puzzled look. The natives have nothing in their experience to which they can relate what is meant by "explosion"; therefore the word is meaningless for them.

This little illustration should make it clear that the Christian *cannot* explain to the non-Christian who God is.

The power of God just is not part of the non-Christian's experience. Experience of who God is can only be gained by faith through the Holy Spirit, who works in man by means of the Word of God. Only through faith can there be true knowledge of God; without the knowledge of faith, man cannot understand God's revelation either. Man's experience, then, is limited to what God has enabled him to know and learn within the created universe.

> The unspiritual man does not receive the gifts of the Spirit of God, for they are folly to him, and he is not able to understand them because they are spiritually discerned (I Cor. 2:14).

The Christian, on the other hand, knows that God is the sovereign Creator of *all* that exists in heaven and on earth. From the Bible—and not from research in, or an understanding of, creation—the Christian knows that God is eternal and is present everywhere at the same time. God is above the limits of man's created mind, and any attempt to prove or understand God's existence from within man's position as a created being is doomed to failure.

The Christian knows that the triune God, Father, Son, and Holy Spirit, created the whole universe, including man. But even the Christian can only get a small glimpse, a cloudy image, of God, for the saved Christian, too, is bound within God's laws by which all things, including thought processes (reason), exist. Neither can man's language and comprehension, which are also part of created reality, express anything that transcends creation except by the Spirit—and then only to those who possess the Spirit as explained in I Corinthians 2:12-13:

> Now we have received not the spirit of the world, but the Spirit which is from God, that we might understand the gifts bestowed on us by God. And we impart this in words not taught by human wisdom but taught by the Spirit, in-

terpreting spiritual truths to those who possess the Spirit.

Man's knowledge of God, then, is partial. Man knows God with the limited human understanding of what God has revealed of Himself in the Bible and in creation, as Romans 11:33-6 clearly points out:

> O the depth of the riches and wisdom and knowledge of God! How unsearchable are his judgments and how inscrutable his ways!
> "For who has known the mind of the Lord,
> or who has been his counselor?"
> "Or who has given a gift to him
> that he might be repaid?"
> For from him and through him and to him are all things. To him be glory for ever. Amen.

The Bible is the source from which the believer builds and replenishes his religious knowledge and commitment. As a result of such constant replenishment or refueling, the believer becomes more sharply attuned to what God has revealed in creation. Then, and only then, can the believer begin to see the harmony (though still scarred by sin) and purpose of the creation, which exists to serve and to glorify God.

If a believer accepts that God has revealed Himself in creation in addition to His self-revelation in the Bible, and that God wishes to be served and glorified through the creation, then he will desire an educational system that develops and nurtures a life-style in harmony with that belief.

What is sin?

When God created heaven and earth, there was no sin because "God saw everything that he had made, and behold,

it was very good" (Gen. 1:31). Somehow, in a way not under-
standable to man, sin entered this perfect creation. There
has been much speculation as to how this happened and
why, but such questions are irrelevant in the context of this
book. Man must deal with what is present in creation, and
sin is part of what confronts man. The Bible only reveals
that satan, through the serpent, tempted man into
disobeying God's command, and that man willfully broke
God's covenant (Gen. 3:1-7).

From the context of the story of the fall and the description throughout Scripture of what is evil in the sight of God,
it can be concluded that sin is anything that is contrary to
God's laws as He has revealed them in the Bible and in
creation. In other words, sin is disobedience to the divine
commandments that give true meaning and purpose to life.
These commandments were given by Jesus in Matthew
22:37-40 when He said:

> You shall love the Lord your God with all your heart, and
> with all your soul, and with all your mind. This is the great
> and first commandment. And a second is like it, You shall
> love your neighbor as yourself. On these two command-
> ments depend all the law and the prophets.

What is the meaning of the fall?

When man disobeyed God's commandment by eating
of the forbidden fruit, it was not only man who was defiled.
God made man completely accountable for everything on
earth when He created man. Because of that accountability,
the whole earth was cursed when man disobeyed God and
fell into sin. In Genesis 3:17-19, God said:

> Because you have listened to the voice of your wife,
>   and have eaten of the tree
> of which I commanded you,

"You shall not eat of it,"
cursed is the ground because of you;
    in toil you shall eat of it all the days of your life;
thorns and thistles it shall bring forth to you;
    and you shall eat the plants of the field.
In the sweat of your face
    you shall eat bread
till you return to the ground,
    for out of it you were taken;
you are dust,
    and to dust you shall return.

Therefore, the meaning of the fall is that the world which God made complete and perfect, the world which God made to serve His glory, became cursed because of man's sin. In effect, the whole world died when man sinned. The lifeline of blessing between God and the world, which was totally represented in man, became the deathline of cursing condemnation (John 3:36). The transformation of this direct relationship between God and creation from blessing into cursing is what Genesis 2:17 means by death. That death is also called "the dominion of darkness"; it is existence apart from God under His sentence (Rom. 3:10-20; Col. 1:13).

What is the meaning of redemption?

The only way in which the perverted creation could be restored to its former place of service would be for mankind to return to its life relationship with God. But man was *dead* because of his sin. He could not stand before God. Instead he tried to hide from God (Gen. 3:8).

All things were created by Christ and for Christ (Col. 1:16). Since man had pulled everything down with him into death, only the intervention of a mediator (Savior) between God and man could restore creation. That mediator could be none other than Jesus Christ, for whom and by whom all things exist (Rom. 11:36).

Thus it was Jesus who took the wrath of God upon Himself, and it was Jesus who gave Himself, by the will of the Father, as a ransom for the sin of His people. Romans 8:3-4 gives expression to that grace:

> For God has done what the law, weakened by the flesh, could not do: sending his own Son in the likeness of sinful flesh and for sin, he condemned sin in the flesh, in order that the just requirement of the law might be fulfilled in us, who walk not according to the flesh but according to the Spirit.

Christ did not come to save His people from their sin only. To believe that is to misunderstand the purpose of creation, which is to serve and glorify God. Creation was not made for *man*; rather, man was created to complete the creation for the glory of God. Christ, who is the owner, the reason for creation's existence, took it upon Himself to become man, the new Head, the last Adam of creation. Christ became the new Head through His suffering and death on the cross so that *all* of His creation — excluding satan and his followers* — would again be reconciled to the Father. The Father accepted Christ's sacrifice as full satisfaction for the sin of His people, with the result that creation is *in principle* reconciled to God through the last Adam:

> For in him all the fulness of God was pleased to dwell, and through him to reconcile to himself all things, whether on

---

*It must be noted here that God is also glorified in the eternal destruction of satan and all his followers under the burning wrath of divine justice. Sin and its defilement will be removed from Christ's Kingdom, but just as salvation is eternal for the godly, so is the curse for the ungodly.

earth or in heaven, making peace by the blood of his cross (Col. 1:19-20).

Those who maintain the view that Christ came to earth only to save *souls* are actually saying that the blood of Christ was not sufficient to overcome *all* sin. If Christ had come to save the souls of His people only, then satan would still have claim to the body, creation, and the world. Scripture speaks of Jesus reconciling all of creation back to the glory of the triune God. Romans 8:18-25 speaks about the hope for creation together with the believer when Paul says:

> I consider that the sufferings of this present time are not worth comparing with the glory that is to be revealed to us. For the creation waits with eager longing for the revealing of the sons of God; for the creation was subjected to futility, not of its own will but by the will of him who subjected it in hope; because the creation itself will be set free from its bondage to decay and obtain the glorious liberty of the children of God. We know that the whole creation has been groaning in travail together until now; and not only the creation, but we ourselves, who have the first fruits of the Spirit, groan inwardly as we wait for adoption as sons, the redemption of our bodies. For in this hope we were saved. Now hope that is seen is not hope. For who hopes for what he sees? But if we hope for what we do not see, we wait for it with patience.

This passage indicates that to proclaim that Jesus died on the cross only for the *souls* of His people is in effect a very narrow gospel. Such a gospel is completely focused on man and can easily turn into a type of Humanism.

To be sure, Christ did come to save His people—but not as an end in itself. Christ saves His people to restore them, as the godly line, to their original calling. Jesus did not come to save His people because there was any worth *in them* which was more desirable to God than the whole of God's plan. God's people are saved to be kings and priests in His creation (I Pet. 2:9; Rev. 1:6).

The redemptive work of the Savior gave His people salvation and *in principle* restored creation to its original purpose of serving and glorifying God. Christ's work as mediator has restored to man the ability to fulfill his calling — the calling to have dominion over all creation. The believing Christian falteringly fulfills that calling under the last Adam, Jesus Christ, in the service of the sovereign God. The non-Christian purposefully works out that calling under the old Adam, in the service of the dominion of darkness.

The salvation of man

The redeeming work of Jesus Christ was not for the benefit of man *only*. However, the salvation of man was a *key part* of the redemption through Christ's sacrifice on the cross. Salvation is a free gift of grace worked by the Spirit of the living Word of God by way of rebirth and faith. That salvation is total. Man cannot add anything to it by his works, as Ephesians 2:8-10 makes clear:

> For by grace you have been saved through faith; and this is not your own doing, it is the gift of God — not because of works, lest any man should boast. For we are his workmanship, created in Christ Jesus for good works, which God prepared beforehand, that we should walk in them.

In this passage it can be seen that restoration to a life of good works, for which God had created man in the first place, is *the* necessary response of the believing Christian.

Faith comes by rebirth. Every person called to salvation must be born again through the baptism of the Spirit. Each successive generation brings forth more people who are added to Christ's Church. This world, scarred by sin, will exist until the complete plan of God has been unfolded. That plan of God is not only that the number of the elect will be complete but also that the gospel of the Kingdom of Christ must be preached and lived out by those who accept that gospel, so that this preaching and life-style will be a testimony to the nations until Christ's return (Rom. 8:39; Eph. 2:8-10).

Rebirth means two things. First of all, the reborn person is restored as a living child of God. The death he died because of Adam's original sin and his own daily sins has been taken away (I Cor. 15). Reborn man is still mortal and must experience physical death. But through rebirth in Christ, the believer receives a spirit whereby the mortal body will put on immortality through physical death. Secondly, the reborn person is restored to his ability to fulfill his cultural responsibility, to work in and develop the Kingdom of Christ (Gen. 1:26-8; Rom. 6; Ephesians; Colossians; etc.).

Genesis 1:26-8, where God gives man his task to have dominion over all of creation, is still very much in force today. Contrary to the belief of many, the Bible nowhere states that man's original calling was withdrawn. The Bible only says that after the fall, extra burdens were added (Gen. 3:17-19).

Christ's set of instructions to the apostles just before His ascension into heaven is at heart a republication of the calling of Genesis 1. God's purpose for this earth is fulfilled in Christ. Thus the only ones who can subdue and preserve the earth, enriching it as God intended, are those among all nations who become disciples of Christ and who are baptized through the Holy Spirit. In Matthew 28:20, right after the call to baptize the nations, Christ adds the call: *"and teach them to observe all the commandments I gave you"* (J.B.) That instruction from the Lord Jesus Christ—as further amplified in Romans 8:18-25 and I Corinthians 15:22-8, among other places—means more than a call to save souls.

Christ said that He had not come to take away the law but to fulfill it (Matt. 5:17-20). It was the law, including the command to enrich the earth, that man could no longer fulfill because of his sins. Christ, as Mediator, having suffered the complete punishment of the law, guarantees by His righteousness the fulfillment of everything that the law requires. By *free grace* the believer has the *ability* and the *responsibility* to carry out his cultural task. Free grace means that saved man can stand in the shadow of Christ, the Mediator, before a righteous God without reference to man's own works. Christ intercedes before the Father when His people fail in their responsibility to love God above all and their neighbors as themselves (Matt. 22:37-40).

2
The Kingdom of Christ
and
the Dominion of Satan

The whole universe exists under the sovereignty of the Creator King. Man, the image-bearer of God, was placed in God's Kingdom to develop that Kingdom and have dominion over it. However, when Adam and Eve wanted to be like God, they transformed themselves and mankind into the ungodly line. As a result of their disobedience, God inflicted upon man and creation the curse of the dominion of satan.

It was discussed earlier that in Christ, creation and the godly line have been restored *in principle* to their original purpose and task. The emphasis must fall on the words *in principle*, since God's people and creation will not be perfected by the last Adam, Christ, until the day of resurrection.

Satan and the rest of the fallen angels were cast out of heaven at the time of Christ's ascension (Rev. 12:1-17). The only remaining power of satan is his constant attempt to destroy Christ's people by making war "on those who keep the commandments of God and bear testimony to Jesus." Until the time of Christ's satisfaction of God's justice and until Christ ascended into heaven, satan was able to accuse the faithful before God day and night (Job 1:6-12; 2:1-6; Zech. 3:1-2; Rev. 12:10). Now, however, satan can only work out his rage at losing the crucial battle in heaven by a final attempt to destroy the godly line—Christ's Church. Satan knows that his final attempt to destroy the Church is doomed to fail. He knows that Jesus Christ will ultimately purge this earth of all evil, casting satan and his people, the ungodly line, into outer darkness so that Christ can deliver His completed Kingdom to the Father (I Cor. 15:24).

Thus, within the total Kingdom of God, there are two kingdoms in the world today. The one is the Kingdom of Christ, and the other is the kingdom of satan. By the fact that all men are children of Adam, all men are also members of the kingdom of satan. Since Adam was accountable for all of creation, he had taken the whole creation with him into the service of satan. But Christ, the last Adam, *in principle* redeemed that which was lost, and He has been busy ever since establishing and developing His Kingdom "until He has put all his enemies under his feet" (I Cor. 15:25).

From the foregoing it can be seen that those who say that Christ has not redeemed creation because satan still has his kingdom in the world believe what is incorrect. People who make that kind of statement have understood neither the purpose of creation nor the plan of redemption. When Christ returns on judgment day to claim fully what is already His *in principle*, His total redemptive plan will have been fulfilled. Christ's redemptive plan is to bring creation to its full development, including man's peculiar task within that creation, and to bring to Himself, by means of His Word proclaimed by believers, all those who have been called to salvation, including those who are yet to be born.

The Kingdom vision is not heaven on earth

The view of Christ's redemption of all creation does not present a vision of a possible heaven on earth here and now.

There can be no heaven on earth while the battle with satan is still raging. The kingdom of satan does not allow the Christian's mortal nature to escape its clutches. Though satan cannot overcome Christ's claim on the Christian as body and soul, God nevertheless allows satan to continue his temptations and deceptions. The battle between the Kingdom of Christ and the kingdom of satan is taking place within the people of God. Each believer experiences that battle. Paul gives expression to that battle as he writes in Romans 7:14-25:

> We know that the law is spiritual; but I am carnal, sold under sin. I do not understand my own actions. For I do not do what I want, but I do the very thing I hate. Now if I do what I do not want, I agree that the law is good. So then it is no longer I that do it, but sin which dwells within me. For I know that nothing good dwells within me, that is, in my flesh. I can will what is right, but I cannot do it. For I do not do the good I want, but the evil I do not want is what I do. Now if I do what I do not want, it is no longer I that do it, but sin which dwells within me.
>
> So I find it to be a law that when I want to do right, evil lies close at hand. For I delight in the law of God, in my inmost self, but I see in my members another law at war with the law of my mind and making me captive to the law of sin

which dwells in my members. Wretched man that I am!
Who will deliver me from this body of death? Thanks be to
God through Jesus Christ our Lord! So then, I of myself
serve the law of God with my mind, but with my flesh I
serve the law of sin.

Man's task in Christ's Kingdom

The emphasis placed on man's task in Christ's redemptive plan should not be interpreted to mean that there is
some *worth* in man which Christ *needs* to complete His
redemptive work. Christ's blood on the cross was all-
sufficient. The passage quoted from Romans 7 shows that
man has no worth in himself. Christ also does not *need* man,
but He *uses* man in His plan of salvation and redemption
just as man was intended to be used in the Genesis mandate.
(See again Chapter 1 — on "The salvation of man.")

The Church in Christ's Kingdom

Christ calls His Church (the body of all true believers)
His Bride. This signifies a marriage relationship. In the
Biblical concept of marriage, the partners become a unity
working toward a common goal. The Bride's side of that
working unity is one of anticipation of what is to come when
the Groom returns. But the love of the Groom for His Bride
is patient and kind. That love never comes to an end. No
matter how often the Bride fails in her calling and responsibilities to build the Kingdom of Christ, the Groom endures
such failures and covers them with love. Paul, in I Corinthians 13:8-12, gives an explanation which shows that the
believer performs his tasks as a mirror image of what is to
come in the new heaven and the new earth when he states:

Love never ends; as for prophecies, they will pass away; as for tongues, they will cease; as for knowledge, it will pass away. For our knowledge is imperfect and our prophecy is imperfect; but when the perfect comes, the imperfect will pass away. When I was a child, I spoke like a child, I thought like a child, I reasoned like a child; when I became a man, I gave up childish ways. For now we see in a mirror dimly, but then face to face. Now I know in part; then I shall understand fully, even as I have been fully understood.

In the parable of the talents, Christ shows that the believer must obediently develop the gifts and talents he has received. In this life, the believer is to use and develop his God-given talents in preparation for the life which is to come in the new heaven and the new earth (Matt. 25). Thus the believer's present life is building the way of peace which leads up to and is approved in the judgment and which continues for all eternity.

While Christ's redemptive plan is being fulfilled, satan knows that his time is running out. He tries everything in his power to save his dominion. Satan is able to destroy much. He has his own evil inventions. While the Bridegroom, Jesus Christ, is in heaven preparing a place and task for His Bride, the Church, satan still tries to deceive God's people in many ways (II John, vs. 7-10). But despite satan's plans and actions, the Church, with the help of the Holy Spirit, is moving to its God-glorifying goal.

God the Holy Spirit

The Holy Spirit, the third person of the Holy Trinity, was sent by the Father after Christ's resurrection and ascension into heaven. In John 14:16-17 and 26, Christ had promised that the Father would send the Holy Spirit. That promise was fulfilled in Acts 2:1-13.

It is the Holy Spirit who works faith in man by means of the reading and proclamation of the Word of God. It is the Holy Spirit who works rebirth in man and who seals baptism to the believer (John 3:5-6). The water of baptism is a sign and seal (a symbol) of the *cleansing power* of the Holy Spirit which man can receive *only* as a result of Christ's death on the cross (Rom. 6:3-4). Baptism symbolizes man's nature dying with Christ on the one hand, while the resurrection of Christ is symbolized by rebirth through the Holy Spirit on the other hand.

When the Holy Spirit was first poured out at Pentecost, His coming was visible in three special, physical ways. The disciples gathered in Jerusalem on the day of Pentecost *heard* His presence, which was like a powerful wind. They *saw* the presence of the Holy Spirit in the form of tongues like fire. In addition, as the Holy Spirit filled them, they began to *speak in foreign languages*. The Holy Spirit gave the apostles an instant knowledge of all the foreign languages they would need. The confusion of Babel, which presented language barriers thwarting the gospel, was in one moment overcome by the Holy Spirit. In this way the Holy Spirit prepared the apostles for their worldwide mission.

After Christ's victory over the kingdom of satan and after His ascension into heaven, Christ wants the Good News to be spread abroad rapidly. In a very short time, the Holy Spirit trains and teaches the disciples the complete truth so that the young Church can be scattered abroad to establish the Kingdom of Christ among all nations.

Since the complete truth taught by the Holy Spirit was recorded in the New Testament by the apostles and since Christ's Church has already been established, the special gifts of the Holy Spirit, namely, *hearing* the wind of His presence, *seeing* the tongues as of fire, and the instant *speaking of foreign languages* without having been trained in them, are no longer needed. Christ's complete redemptive plan has been revealed in the Word of God and is available to everyone—particularly in this hemisphere. In short, the Holy Spirit now uses orderly, normative ways to nurture and educate the believer towards growth in faith and knowledge of the complete truth.

By the grace of Christ, the Holy Spirit is very active in North America. He convinces man of his sin and of God's righteousness in judging unrepentant sinners, damning them to eternal misery and sorrow. But when the convicted sinner sees no other way out, the Holy Spirit baptizes the sinner with Himself to a new life in the service of the Kingdom of Christ. That baptism of the Holy Spirit is *not seen* in the speaking in tongues, but it *is seen* in a life lived in obedience to Christ's command to love God above all and one's neighbor as oneself. The Holy Spirit, then, sanctifies the reborn child of God by setting the believer apart and preparing him for *productive service* in the Kingdom of Christ.

> But you are a chosen race, a royal priesthood, a holy nation, God's own people, that you may declare the wonderful deeds of him who called you out of darkness into his marvelous light (I Pet. 2:9).

The preparation for that task is an ongoing thing in this life and will only be complete when Christ returns for the last time to change the reborn into immortality at the triumph of the resurrection. At that time the Christian will be completely ready to take up his task in the new heaven and on the new earth.

The need for Christian education

Christian education is important for every Christian who understands that the battle between the Kingdom of

Christ and the kingdom of satan takes place within the believer. Christian education becomes a necessity for everyone who sees and accepts in addition that this life leads to the triumph of the resurrection. In a Christian school, a child's talents can be developed—with the help of the Holy Spirit—toward present and future service in the Kingdom of Christ.

The Christian school is in a setting where the curriculum can constantly be tested and reformed in accordance with the Word of God under the guidance of the Holy Spirit. That does not mean that there is perfection in the Christian school. On the contrary, the battle between the two opposing kingdoms also takes place within the Christian school. But at least there *is* a battle. In a school system where God's authority is not recognized, there may be strife, but no battle for the complete truth takes place because the fundamental religious direction is service in the kingdom of satan. The seemingly calm and disciplined atmosphere in many schools can be very deceptive. One must always test the spirit of the educational content, scope and direction (i.e. the curriculum) to see if *it* is directed to the service of Christ or of satan.

The call to be set apart and to be prepared for a productive life of service applies particularly to education. A large part of the child's development and learning takes place in the school. Therefore the Christian should keep in mind what the Word of God says in II Corinthians 6:12—7:1:

> You are not restricted by us, but you are restricted in your own affections. In return—I speak as to children—widen your hearts also.
> Do not be mismated with unbelievers. For what partnership have righteousness and iniquity? Or what fellowship has light with darkness? What accord has Christ with Belial? Or what has a believer in common with an unbeliever?

What agreement has the temple of God with idols? For we
are the temple of the living God; as God said,

"I will live in them and move among them,
and I will be their God,
and they shall be my people.
Therefore come out from them,
and be separate from them, says the Lord,
and touch nothing unclean;
then I will welcome you,
and I will be a father to you,
and you shall be my sons and daughters,
says the Lord Almighty."

Since we have these promises, beloved, let us cleanse ourselves from every defilement of body and spirit, and make
holiness perfect in the fear of God.

3
Faith and Education

The basis of knowledge

The foundation of a Christian's knowledge is faith in the Word of God. In the context of this chapter, it is necessary to explain what is meant by the Word of God. In John 1, Jesus Christ is also called God's Word. Proverbs 8:22-31; Isaiah 55:10-11; John 1; Colossians 1:15-20; and Hebrews 1 also show that creation came into being, and still exists, by the Word of God. God spoke, and it came into being; He commanded, and things appeared in the way God's Word demanded that they appear. It is evident from Scripture that God and the Word are inseparable. Where

God is, there the Word is also. The triune God is *omnipresent*.

John 1:1 says: "In the beginning was the Word, and the Word was with God, and the Word was God." Verses 4 and 5 read: "In him was life, and the life was the light of men. The light shines in the darkness, and the darkness has not overcome it." And again in verse 10: "He was in the world, and the world was made through him, yet the world knew him not." Colossians 1:16-17 states in part: ". . . for in him [Christ] all things were created, in heaven and on earth, visible and invisible . . . and in him all things hold together." Also, Hebrews 1:2-3 says:

> But in these last days he has spoken to us by a Son, whom he appointed the heir of all things, through whom also he created the world. He reflects the glory of God and bears the very stamp of his nature, upholding the universe by his word of power.

The Word of God, then, which comes to focus in the Lord Jesus Christ, has been revealed to man not only in the Bible but also in creation. Romans 1:20 makes that clear beyond a doubt: "Ever since the creation of the world his invisible nature, namely, his eternal power and deity, has been clearly perceived in the things that have been made."

When one understands the Word of God in this way, it *is* correct to say that the Bible is God's Word, but not that God's revelation is the Bible *only*. The Bible itself speaks of this broader revelation of God.

However, the Bible is the only source from which the Christian can discover why and to what end everything exists. The Christian also knows from the Bible that God is faithful, trustworthy, and true to Himself and His laws (Ps. 33; 89; 119:89-91; Is. 25:6). That knowledge is gained not by philosophy or science but by faith in the Word of God as given in the Bible. Only the Bible has been given as the infallible Word of God. Though God has revealed Himself in creation, that creation also carries the curse and defilement of sin. Satan uses that defilement of creation to persuade man to accept the lie as if it were the truth. The Christian's knowledge of faith can be expanded and strengthened by his perceived revelation of God in creation only insofar as that knowledge of faith is in agreement with the revelation of the Bible which at present is the only available *infallible* Word of God. Hebrews 11:3 states: "By faith we understand that the world was created by the word of God, so that what is seen was made out of things which do not appear."

For the Christian, then, faith is a certain knowledge of the things one cannot see; it is unconditional acceptance of what the Bible says about itself, about God, and about creation. Faith is the foundation of the Christian's knowledge not because reason or philosophy convince him but because the Spirit of Light works that faith in the reborn.

The non-Christian's knowledge is also based on faith. His faith in knowledge is based on the unconditional acceptance of reason as the infallible source of truth, not because his research or philosophy can prove that but because the spirit of darkness convinces him. Something created (reason) becomes the non-Christian's god.

The function of education

The function of education is systematically to lead and direct, to foster and train the child to develop and cultivate his body, mind, heart, personality, and behavior for his task in life. The emphasis must be placed on the word *systematically*, for without a methodical approach based on sound principles, there can be only a chaotic dispensing of facts and ideas which the child will not be able to fit into a total picture.

The basis of education

The methods and principles of education are influenced by the knowledge of who man *is* and the purpose and cause of his existence. But that knowledge of man's being and the purpose for his existence is a knowledge which cannot be acquired through science or philosophy; it can only be known by faith. For if one believes that man exists purely by chance as the result of some unexplainable process of evolution, then one's theories, philosophies, methodologies, and activities will be built by oneself, upon oneself, around oneself, with no other foundation than that. On the other hand, the Christian believes that man was created by God for the purpose of being His servant in creation. Since the Christian begins with that foundation, he constructs all his theories, philosophies, methodologies, and activities beneath the sovereignty of God.

The Christian's purpose for education is to nurture the child to glorify, worship, and serve the sovereign Creator. The non-Christian's basis and purpose for education will be to glorify, worship and serve something in creation. By faith, out of his own understanding, the non-Christian chooses something within creation to explain his origin and existence. That understanding then becomes his religion, which he must believe in and live by. The theory of evolution, for instance, is an example of such a faith-commitment to a theory.

From the foregoing, it must be concluded that *all education is religious education*. The idea that the basis, purpose, methods, and principles of education can be neutral is a myth. That myth is planted and fostered in the mind of man by the spirit of darkness.

The choice in education

There are basically only two types of education to choose from, namely, Christian and non-Christian education. The concept that all education is religious education leaves only the choice of which type of religious education the child should receive.

This does not mean that the choice of the type of education will be a clear-cut, black-and-white type of choice. Unfortunately, the choice is much more difficult because there are many shades of gray between the two alternatives.

Some conceive of Christian education as adding Jesus Christ, Bible reading and prayer to the public school curriculum. They do not see that the core curriculum — including reading, writing and arithmetic — should be any different in a Christian school than in a non-Christian school.

On the other end of the scale are the supporters of separate Christian education who believe that the basic faith-commitment of the school or the system affects the approach and content of all subject matter. These people are convinced that a *systematic* approach to developing and cultivating the whole child, i.e. his body, mind, heart, personality, and behavior, causes all subjects to be interwoven. Such Christians also believe that the faith-commitment and life system presented to them in Scripture determines to a large extent the principles and methods of education. (Although the mechanical aspects of the core subjects may be the same for everyone, the rationale may not.) These Christians maintain that the child must be taught, for example, that 2 + 2 always comes out to 4 — not as a result of man's logic or of the creative mind or as a fluke of nature but because that is evidence of God's faithfulness and trustworthiness towards His creation.

In the non-Christian schools there is also a range of

choices. There are schools in communities which are almost wholly made up of Christian residents. These schools, although they are public, non-Christian schools, will give some form of recognition to Christian values. They may even include Bible reading and prayer. At the other end of the range of non-Christian education is the school in which both God's authority and existence are denied.

In the choice of a school for the child, one must also consider the selection and hiring of teachers. The teacher, after all, has a direct influence on the child. If the teacher is not a committed Christian, he or she cannot present the subject matter in a Christian way.

One of the biggest dangers in a non-Christian school, even in an almost completely Christian community, is that the Christian community has no control over the hiring of teachers. One year the child may have a teacher who is indeed a dedicated Christian; the next year he may have a professed non-Christian for a teacher. Such a teacher may agree to partake in the "ritual" of morning devotions; the rest of the school day, however, is subtly used to make those devotions a mockery.

The supporting community of the Christian school is more directly involved in the hiring of teachers. As members of the school society operating the school, they elect the board which hires the staff. By constitutional requirement, teachers in most Christian schools must be confessing Christians who give evidence of a Christian life-style. It is safe to say that without that constitutional safeguard and without the direct say of the supporting community in the choice and hiring of teachers, it would be difficult—if not impossible—to have and maintain Christian education. In the chapter on *Education and the Family*, this statement will receive further discussion.

The result of education

In view of the foregoing, the question of which school to choose for the child will have to be answered on the basis of which school operates on the foundation of faith in the truth of the Word of God. Education which is based on *that* kind of faith honors and serves the sovereign God. Education which is of man, by man, for man — based on the autonomy of man's reason — honors and serves the dominion of satan.

Christ demands that Christians serve Him in their total life. In Matthew 22:37-40, Christ gives the summary of the law of Moses as loving God completely with heart, soul and mind and loving one's neighbor as oneself. Education which does not obey that summary is not service to Christ, even if that education is nominally Christian.

The result of not teaching the child according to the Lord's summary of the law is given by Jesus Christ in Matthew 5:17-20:

> Think not that I have come to abolish the law and the prophets; I have come not to abolish them but to fulfil them. For truly, I say to you, till heaven and earth pass away, not an iota, not a dot, will pass from the law until all is accomplished. Whoever then relaxes one of the least of these commandments and teaches men so, shall be called least in the kingdom of heaven; but he who does them and teaches them shall be called great in the kingdom of heaven. For I tell you, unless your righteousness exceeds that of the scribes and Pharisees, you will never enter the kingdom of heaven.

The consequence of a Christian family sending the child to a non-Christian school which denies the sovereignty of God is more severe. There is no better way to explain this than to quote what Paul said in Romans 1:18-32:

> For the wrath of God is revealed from heaven against all ungodliness and wickedness of men who by their wicked-

ness suppress the truth. For what can be known about God is plain to them, because God has shown it to them. Ever since the creation of the world his invisible nature, namely, his eternal power and deity, has been clearly perceived in the things that have been made. So they are without excuse; for although they knew God they did not honor him as God or give thanks to him, but they became futile in their thinking and their senseless minds were darkened. Claiming to be wise, they become fools, and exchange the glory of the immortal God for images resembling mortal man or birds or animals or reptiles.

Therefore God gave them up in the lusts of their hearts to impurity, to the dishonoring of their bodies among themselves, because they exchanged the truth about God for a lie and worshiped and served the creature rather than the Creator, who is blessed for ever! Amen.

For this reason God gave them up to dishonorable passions. Their women exchanged natural relations for unnatural, and the men likewise gave up natural relations with women and were consumed with passion for one another, men committing shameless acts with men and receiving in their own persons the due penalty for their error.

And since they did not see fit to acknowledge God, God gave them up to a base mind and to improper conduct. They were filled with all manner of wickedness, evil, covetousness, malice. Full of envy, murder, strife, deceit, malignity, they are gossips, slanderers, haters of God, insolent, haughty, boastful, inventors of evil, disobedient to parents, foolish, faithless, heartless, ruthless. Though they know God's decree that those who do such things deserve to die, they not only do them but approve those who practice them.

This passage shows the results of education based on faith in man's reason.

Evangelism in education

The opinion is often expressed that children of

Christian families ought to be sent to the non-Christian public school so they may be a Christian witness there. Such sentiments, which may appear laudable, are based on a number of faulty assumptions.

First of all, the notion that a child from a Christian home can witness in a non-Christian educational setting presupposes that the child (aside from the assumption that he is already born again) has achieved some level of Christian maturity. This alone is an assumption most organized Christian churches are not even prepared to make of the youth of their own congregations.

Although it is accepted in Christian churches that the Holy Spirit does not restrict baptism of the Holy Spirit, or rebirth, to any specific age level, children must nevertheless show evidence of faith and acquire a certain level of Biblical understanding before they are allowed to be baptized or to confess their faith to become full church members. Thus, adult baptism or confirmation by confession of faith seldom takes place before the teenage years; in many denominations it does not take place until the end of the teenage years.

If the organized church recognizes and requires the need for a certain level of maturity in the child before he or she may become a full communicant member, how can that same child be expected to give sound Christian witness in a non-Christian setting? The chances are rather that that non-Christian teacher will influence the Christian child — more, if not less — toward the non-Christian view of life than that the immature child will influence the teacher and his classmates. This does not mean that God does not sometimes use children with their childlike sincerity to do just that, but such a thing would be the exception rather than the rule.

The second faulty assumption concerns the function of education. The function of education in the school setting is not to evangelize but to develop and cultivate the child's total life to take up his calling in life.

The primary responsibility of the home is to provide food and shelter and to nurture the child in the fear of the Lord. (See the chapter on *Education and the Family*.) The primary educational task of the church is to nurture the child in God's revelation in the Bible as articulated in the church doctrines. The primary function of the school is to nurture the child in God's revelation in creation. Although the church and the school have primary responsibility in their own area, both continue and strengthen the nurture of the home. If one of these three Christian nurturing institutions is replaced with a non-Christian one, the child is not nurtured in obedience to God's total revelation and laws.

Christian parents should reread Matthew 5:17-19 and Romans 1:18-32 on the possible consequences of not providing their children with a unified, consistent nurturing foundation.

4
Education and the Family

This chapter will not be an in-depth discussion of what the family is and how all the family's members relate to one another. Such a discussion would fall outside the scope of this book. The purpose here is to demonstrate how education and the family relate to each other.

In an earlier chapter, it was stated that the primary responsibility of the home is to provide food and shelter and to nurture the child in the fear of the Lord. In Deuteronomy Moses makes it very plain that children are to be taught the whole law from a very early age (Deut. 4:9-10; 6:4-9).

The child is born into the institution of the family. It is in the family, therefore, that the child first interacts with other human beings. In the family setting, the child is to be obedient to the instructions of the parents. The parents are to bring up, correct, and guide the child in a way that will not drive him to resentment (Eph. 6:4). The parents are to nurture their child in the way the Lord has revealed Himself to be—loving, patient, and trustworthy. Christian parents must nurture their child to understand God's law so that the child will take his place within the Kingdom of Christ. (See Chapter 1—the section on "What is the meaning of redemption?")

The family, however, is not able to satisfy all the educational needs of the child in today's complex society. Life is more specialized today, and the family has given up many of the tasks it used to perform. Today there are various institutions, such as the state, the church, the school, and the business enterprise. Though it makes rules and engages in discipline, the family is not the state. And though it worships as family, the family is not the church. In the same way, though it nurtures the child, the family is not the school.

The family expects the school first of all to take care of the greater part of formal education—the education which deals primarily with God's revelation in creation. The family expects the visible church first of all to teach Scripture and the doctrines found in it. The family itself leads and directs the child to obey and worship God and to walk in the fear of the Lord. The Bible is read and used by the school, the church, and the family as a source of regeneration, insight and inspiration rather than as a textbook.

On the basis of Deuteronomy 6, it can be seen that the family has the primary accountability for all aspects of nurturing. In spite of the fact that the family has been relieved of part of the *task* of nurturing, the family remains *accountable* to God for what the child is taught and what he learns in both church and school.

In Chapter 3, the section on "The choice in education,"

the statement was made that "without the direct say of the supporting community·in the choice and hiring of teachers, it would be difficult — if not impossible — to have and maintain Christian education." This supporting community consists of families whose children are students at the school *in particular* and members of the family of Christ *in general* (Matt. 12:50). In the Biblical concept, the nucleus family — parents and children, natural and adopted, young and mature — has *particular accountability*, and the members of the family of Christ (all Christian believers with whom the nucleus family interacts in a given location) have *general supportive responsibility* to assist the nucleus family. For this reason, most of the Christian schools which are part of the International Union of Christian Schools quite correctly count their membership by families in particular and by supporting members in general.

Accountable authority-responsibility

Of course students do not have authority in the school, even though they are family members. The role of the students in a school is the same as that of children in a family. The role of children is different from that of the parents in the family. Parents are the members of the family who are charged to lead and direct their children. That is the authority-responsibility for which parents are accountable to God. As parents lead and direct their children, their children become more and more responsible to their parents and accountable to God. In the same way, students in the school become more and more accountable to God as they mature and become responsible to those who are charged to lead and direct them. Authority, responsibility, and accountability are not the same. To lead and direct is to exercise *authority*; to learn and respond is to exercise *responsibility*;

and to obey and subject oneself to God is to exercise *account-ability*. These are the three distinct but complementary meanings in the Biblical sense. Therefore one must speak of *accountable authority-responsibilities* when referring to human interrelationships in any situation.*

The purpose of this chapter is not to deal with the question of *accountable authority-responsibility* within the classroom. That question will be dealt with in Part II of this book, when the relationship between God, parents, teachers, students, and community will be discussed in more detail. The purpose here is to point out that the *account-ability* for all nurture rests with the family and that *this ac-countability can never be delegated*. For this reason, the nucleus family, in particular, and the family of Christ, in

---

*To regain the Biblically faithful understanding of the *ac-countable authority-responsibility* concept, it is necessary to reject the common definitions of the words *authority*, *responsibility*, and *accountability*. The common meanings of these words are distorted because they proceed from the man-centered concept of life and the universe. The man-centered view necessarily subverts the meaning of authority from the Christian concept of being charged to lead and direct beneath the sovereign God to the non-Christian concept of power or right to control. In that non-Christian view, accountability and responsibility are reduced from two distinct concepts (i.e. accountability operates because of the command to love God above all, while responsibility operates because of the command to love the neighbor as oneself) to one concept for both words. Since the non-Christian does not recognize God's authority, accountability has to operate in obedience to the "god-man" and becomes equated with responsibility. This "god-man" is accountable and responsible ultimately only to his own authority. In the Christian concept, on the other hand, authority *never* operates apart from responsibility, though responsibility may operate without authority. Authority and responsibility *both* operate in conjunction with accountability to the sovereign God.

general, which together make up the school society's membership, must exercise leadership and direction over the operation and policy development of the Christian school. If this direct involvement is removed, the Biblically faithful understanding of *accountable authority-responsibility* is rejected. In such a case, the healthy interaction, interrelationship and interdependence between home, school and Christian community is lost. The result of rejecting the Biblical meaning of authority, responsibility and accountability and leaving the hiring, policy development and operation of the school to an administrative bureaucracy can be seen in most non-Christian public schools.

5
The Relationship between Church, School and State

What is the church?

In the previous chapter on the family, it was said that the discussion of the nature of the family was outside the scope of this book. That is also the case with the church. In the context of this chapter, the primary concern is with the relationship of education to the local congregations or denominations and also to the total body of Christ. (The Church as the body of Christ is not confined to any one denomination or local congregation.) In earlier chapters (especially Chapter 2), it has been pointed out that the

Church as body of Christ ought to be involved in education — but not the church as denomination or local congregation.

Before that statement is further clarified, it will be necessary to have a clear understanding of what is meant by the state and its task.

What is the state?

In the previous chapter, the observation was made that in more primitive times, the family carried out most of the cultural tasks. There was no need for the institution of the state in those days. The Biblical account of the time from Abraham to the crossing of the river Jordan by the people of Israel to take possession of the promised land presents a picture of growing complexity — from extended family (including servants as part of the family) through the tribal period to full nationhood.

The state, then, resulted from the development and unfolding of God's plan for creation. At first the church and the state were very much intertwined. The judges of Israel, as well as David and Solomon, concerned themselves with the task of confessing and worshiping in its institutional form as well as with codifying and applying just laws. However, in the time of King Jehoshaphat (II Chron. 19), the separation between the confessional and political tasks in the young nation of Judah already became distinguishable in a somewhat formalized way. The temple and the palace became more and more separated as far as their peculiar tasks were concerned.

It became the task of the state to deal with the area of justice. Jehoshaphat said to the judges he appointed:

Consider what you do, for you judge not for man but for

the Lord; he is with you in giving judgment. Now then, let
the fear of the Lord be upon you; take heed what you do,
for there is no perversion of justice with the Lord our God, or
partiality, or taking bribes (II Chron. 19:6-7).

The state receives authority from God to administer justice
in complete impartiality and in obedience to the Law as
summarized in Deuteronomy 6:1-13, and later confirmed by
Christ in Matthew 22:37-40. That mandate defines the task
of the state even today.

Relation of church and state

In the introductory chapter of this book, the North
American concept of separation between church and state
was briefly reviewed. It was shown that the original division
between the organized church and the state became a
division between the Church as the body of Christ and the
state. The Christian forefathers of the two major North
American nations were not wrong in recognizing the distinct
tasks of the institutions of church and state, as long as they
remembered that these two institutions were both under the
sovereign lordship of God. However, former generations
went wrong when they understood the task of the state as
having control over every area of life not directly related to
the task of preaching, the administration of the sacraments,
and the church polity of the organized church.

The greatest error in the overextended concept of the
state was that the founding fathers lost sight of the origin of
both church and state. In the foregoing it was shown that
both church and state came into existence as a result of the
development and unfolding of society. The tasks of both
church and state were appointed by God, who is sovereign
over all. In accepting the concept that either the church or
the state is the center of authority, the family as a distinct in-

stitution and as a center of authority accountable directly to God was first overlooked, and then forgotten. The import of the cultural, historical development of church and state was obscured, as both church and state stopped following the sound Old Testament practice of counting membership by families.

It was not an accident or coincidence that the Christian communities which were first to regain an understanding of the claim of Jesus Christ on all areas of life were those which had rejected the exclusive church-state authority concept. Those communities continued to count their membership by families. In that way they gave evidence of their high regard for the original cultural institution of the family. Thereby they acknowledged that the family was an authority-responsibility center which God had appointed as equal to the church and the state, and also that all three, (i.e. church, state and family) are under the all-encompassing sovereignty of God.

Around the turn of the century, helped by the insights of European Biblical scholars and statesmen, some Christian communities, illuminated by Scripture, found deep insight into their own complex society in the covenant history of the Old Testament. They saw that one institution should not lord it over another, but that all institutions should operate side by side under the *one* authority of the Word of God. These Christian communities saw that though all institutions are interrelated, one does not have authority over the other.

That unique but interrelated concept of all institutions means simply that while each institution is to some extent involved in what other institutions do, each has its own *primary task* for which it receives authority-responsibility directly from God. That primary authority-responsibility is to be worked out in co-responsibility with the primary authority-responsibility of every other institution. All the authority-responsibility centers are co-accountable to the sovereign God who has charged each institution with its peculiar task. That concept has been called *sphere-sovereignty*.

A few examples of that *primary task* concept should help us understand the Reformed outlook that is characteristic of most schools which are members of the International Union. Those who accept the Reformed view explain that the church, in addition to its primary task of proclaiming the Word of God (its confessional task), maintains church polity and discipline (administers justice), collects money to conduct its own business (economic activity), teaches doctrines (educational activity), etc. Likewise the state, in addition to its primary task of maintaining order through just laws (administering justice), also conducts state business (economic activity), educates the nation to understand and interpret laws and regulations (educational activity), proclaims its authority to exist (confessional activity), etc.

For Christians who accept the foregoing view, the relation between church and state is quite clear. They, like the Christian forefathers of the United States and of Canada, want to see a clear distinction between the task and authority-responsibility of church and state. However, for them the *distinction* of task does not mean the *separation* of the state from what God called it to be. Both church and state must worship and honor the God by whom both exercise authority-responsibility. Denying the requirement of the state to worship and obey God does not make the state neutral. On the contrary, such denial only means that the state bases its authority on some created aspect of reality, such as the democratic process in this age. Basing faith on the democratic process is a modern form of idol worship.

Implication for education

The concepts outlined in Part I of this book do not allow either the church or the state to have control or authority over education. Neither does either church or state have control or authority over the family. Family, church, and state each exist in their own areas to perform their God-given tasks. Under that concept, schools should be neither government-operated nor church-controlled. Christian day schools should be non-denominational and should be operated by families and general members who share the same commitment and subscribe to the same constitution. The constitution expresses the authority-responsibility by which the school society operates. The school society is another authority-responsibility center alongside the home, the church and the state. The school society's authority-responsibility center is to lead and direct its members, young and old, in research, teaching, and learning God's revelation in the Bible and creation. The school society as a whole is accountable to God alone for the way it discharges that task.

Again it must be stated that although the Reformed view does not accept the control of authority of the state over education, this does not mean that the government has no responsibility in relation to the operation of schools. Governments, as part of their task to do justice, must see to it that some basic standards of education are met. And if the state gives grants for the education of children, it must let such grants follow the child to whatever school the child attends. If the state does not do that, it is not impartially dispensing justice (II Chron. 19:7).

However, it is inconsistent to appeal to the United Nations Declaration of Human Rights, Section 26(3), when Christian school supporters request full recognition and tax support for their alternate religious form of education. The relevant section states that:

> Parents have the *prior right* to choose the kind of education that shall be given their children (emphasis mine—DLK).

The problem with that statement is the appeal to *prior right*, which is clearly meant to center in *man's* autonomous choice. If it is a matter of *man's* choice, then that prior right can be delegated to the state for the common good. On that basis most governments will assert correctly that the United Nations Declaration does not conflict with their concept of democratically delegated control over education. The appeal for recognition and just tax support for the alternate Reformed Christian schools is only valid on the deeply religious conviction of *accountability* to the sovereign Lord for the *charge* He has given Christians to nurture their children in the true knowledge of God. It must be made clear that it is impossible to delegate a charge which one has *no right* to delegate without incurring the punishment of disobedience. The Reformed Christian school supporter views the disobedience to that *charge* from His sovereign Lord as equivalent to a soldier's disobeying a command of his commanding officer during wartime. Such an act is punishable by death.

It must also be made clear that Reformed Christian education is not the result of dissatisfaction with the *quality* of "academic" education in the public schools—if by "academic" education is meant the basic curriculum and quality of presentation as required by state or provincial government regulations. Reformed Christian education exists solely to integrate "academic" education with a total view of life for the advancement of, and in obedience to, the true knowledge of God. From one point of view, parents and supporters of that alternate form of education already have the *benefits* of "academic" education available to them since they pay all public education taxes. From that point of view, the *benefits* of Reformed Christian education are *solely* religious. From another point of view, it can be argued that the benefits of Reformed Christian education are both religious and "academic." From that point of view, *no benefits* accrue as a result of the payment of taxes for the "academic" education of the public school system. It is impossible to argue consistently that the *same* "academic" benefits or advantages can accrue twice. Thus, it must be logically concluded that *either* the payment of direct and indirect taxes to the municipal or regional education system is a payment for which no right, privilege, benefit, or advantage accrues, *or* that all payments to Reformed Christian education societies are without any of these rights, privileges, benefits, or advantages. Both *cannot* be true at the same time.

Part II

Reformed Christian Schools

and the

International Union of

Christian Schools

*This is a story about
unique schools where
discovering God's world
is part of a strong system
oriented to values
and norms.*

6

*It is a story about
Reformed Christian schools.*

*From earliest childhood,
parents are involved
with the education
of their children.*

Once the children are old enough to go to school, parents must decide which school they should attend.

The public school . . .

the church-operated school . . .

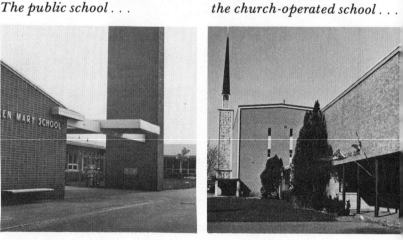

*Today
thousands of students
are attending
interdenominational
Christian schools . . .*

or the Christian school.

*and their numbers are rapidly increasing
as parents decide that
the alternate and independent Christian school
is the only choice for their children.*

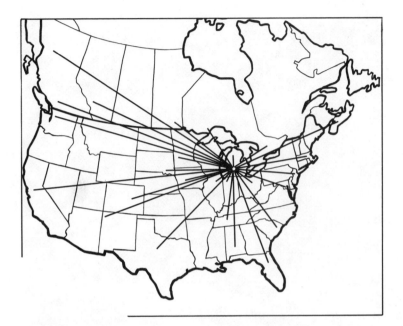

Well over three hundred of these Christian schools
have been organized into a service organization
called the International Union of Christian Schools.

*In a Reformed Christian school,
a Christian nurture program teaches the student
who he is and how he relates to God, others and the world . . .*

*through a curriculum
including language studies and communications;
social studies; math and sciences; and Bible studies,
including a look at other religious systems.*

At a Christian school, discovery is only part of the process. After discovery comes response.

At a Reformed Christian school, all things fall into place because Christ is acknowledged as the Lord of creation and the source of meaning in an otherwise confusing world of events, facts and emotions.

*At a Reformed Christian
school there is a
sharpening of skills,
preparation for work
and personal growth.*

*The Reformed Christian school can help make communities
better places to live because its students have caught
a glimpse of what it means to be Christian citizens.*

*Students at a Christian school
learn that man is
accountable to God
for what he does in the world.*

*Reformed
Christian schools
offer education
which provides
continuity
between
home and church.*

*The teachers in Reformed Christian schools
are dedicated Christians
who develop and use curriculum materials
with a unique Christian perspective.*

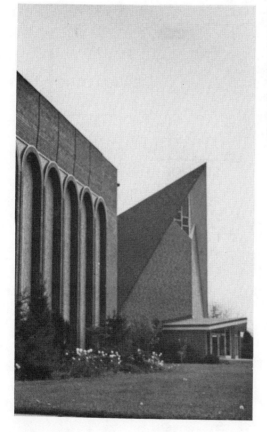

*Reformed
Christian schools
are not
denominational
schools, nor
do they give
denominational
indoctrination.*

Christian education involves interaction between all the members of a Christian community. Supporting Christian education is an investment in the growth of the Church of Jesus Christ.

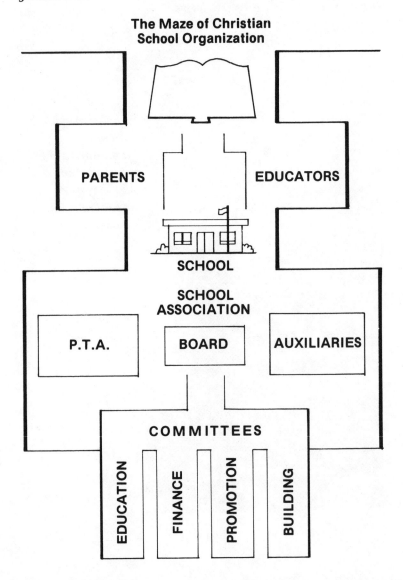

The Maze of Christian School Organization

7
The Reformed Christian School

What is a Reformed Christian school society?

A Reformed Christian school society is not a school society which is operated by a particular denomination or one whose members necessarily come from Reformed churches. A Reformed Christian school society is not church controlled, but is based on the view of life and the world presented in Part I of this book.

By way of summary, it can be stated that a Reformed Christian school society will subscribe to the following principles.

(1)   The Bible, as the infallible, authoritative Word of

89

God in both Old and New Testament, must be accepted in faith as the rule for all of life, including educational activity.

(2)   The sovereignty of God means that the triune God is in control of the whole universe and all that takes place in it. God has not abandoned the creation to satan. Instead God reveals Himself and His majesty in all creation, redeeming it (except for satan and his followers) by Jesus Christ after man brought the curse of sin on all creation. The Christian student, therefore, can glorify God as he seeks to know God by developing the potential found in himself and the creation.

(3)   Knowing the covenant relationship between God and man is essential to understanding the purpose of man's existence. God established His covenant of creation (the covenant of His favor) with man when He commanded him to be the obedient head of creation and to develop creation to its fullest potential. God's solemn obligation under that covenant was that man should be blessed if he obeyed God's command and cursed if he broke it. After the fall, God renewed the covenant in grace through the Mediator Jesus Christ, who was born from a virgin. As perfect God and perfect man, but without sin, Christ willingly offered Himself as a substitute for all His people. By His death on the cross, He carried the full wrath of God's righteousness against sin. Christ's work of salvation was complete when, after His resurrection, He ascended into heaven as the first fruit of the redeemed. Jesus Christ now continues His work of redemption and rules the universe from heaven as its Head and King. As a result of Christ's mediation, the believer is again called to his cultural task

until Christ returns to judge the nations.

(4)   God calls every person to a particular task. Every student must be diligently taught God's revelation both in the Bible and in creation so that he will be prepared to acknowledge and accept his calling (in whatever vocation that may be) to the glory of the triune God. If the student does not by faith acknowledge and accept the sovereignty of God in his calling, he will be a covenant breaker subject to all the consequences listed in the Bible.

What is contained in these four points does not exhaust the concepts to which a Reformed Christian school society will subscribe. However, a school society which does not subscribe to these principles can hardly be called a Reformed Christian school society. Such a school society may be Christian, but not in the Calvinistic Reformed tradition. The beauty of the Reformed view of the world and life is that faith is not limited to the confessional aspects of life; it applies equally to the *cultural* aspects. Man is viewed not as a *spiritual* man on the one side and a *natural* man on the other but in body and soul as one *complete* man who in every activity serves either God or an idol.

How can a Reformed Christian school be identified?

A Reformed Christian school can be easily recognized by what is said in the constitution or bylaws of the sponsoring society. The constitution is a document which defines the basis, purpose and structure for the Christian school society along with the principles and specific guidelines for operating the society's school(s) and conducting its other activities.

Most Reformed Christian school societies make

reference in their basis article to Reformed creedal standards. Some of these schools may even identify some specific Reformed creeds. In these cases the intent is not to identify with, or to submit to, the authority of a particular church or denomination. These expressions are sincere attempts to give recognition to the unique Reformed confessional commitment of the society. In these cases, as well as in the case of school societies which do not appeal to specific creedal standards, there is usually a list of specifically Reformed principles which form the basic educational guidelines for the school society.

In addition to the constitution and bylaws, the Reformed Christian school will emphasize the wholeness of life in all the subjects taught. The school's curriculum will emphasize the responsibility of the student (as body and soul) to acquire diligently all the knowledge needed to serve God, His people, and His creation in whatever the student's particular calling may be. That integrated, confessional, cultural emphasis, as outlined in Part I of this book and summarized in the four points at the beginning of this chapter, is unique to the Reformed Christian school society and the operation of its school(s).

Who can be members of
a Reformed Christian school society?

The Reformed Christian school is a non-denominational school. All believing Christians who accept the Bible as the infallible, authoritative Word of God, who believe that man has a societal and cultural task as well as a need for personal salvation and piety, who agree with the basis and purpose articles of the society's constitution or bylaws, and who belong to a church which subscribes to one or more of the Reformed creeds, are eligible for membership in a Reformed Christian school society.

In the chapter on *The Family and Education* in Part I, the emphasis was placed on the need for continuity between the education a child receives at home. at church, and at school. For that reason, most Reformed Christian school societies will normally require that the applicant for membership in the society be a member in good standing of an evangelical orthodox church whose doctrines are in agreement with the basis article of the constitution or bylaws. More specifically, these applicants will be required to be members of a church which accepts one or more of the following creedal standards:

> Heidelberg Catechism
> Belgic Confession of Faith
> Canons of Dort
> The Westminster Confession of Faith and Catechisms
> The Baptist Confession of Faith of 1689 (also called the Philadelphia Confession)
> The Augsburg Confession
> The Thirty-nine Articles

It should be noted that there are some Reformed school societies which either primarily or exclusively limit the membership or the enrolment of students to members of a particular denomination. These school societies will likely agree with the conditions of enrolment and membership presented in these pages, except for the church membership requirement. Again there are variations in this too. Some of these societies will accept students of parents who belong to churches with identical creeds and who promote similar life styles, while others will draw strict denominational lines. The schools operated by such societies, though solidly Reformed in theology and teaching are not transdenominational Reformed Christian schools. Though such school societies are independent from church government or control, they are not non-denominational in scope.

How is a Reformed Christian school operated?

The Reformed Christian school society or association elects a board of directors or trustees which implements the aims, purposes, and policies of the society. The board has the duties, policy-making responsibilities, and authority-responsibility* specified in the constitution. Board members, as elected representatives of the membership, are responsible to the society and accountable to God, and must report regularly to the membership. All budgets, financial statements, policy changes, program changes, and major curriculum changes are referred to the annual or semiannual meetings of the society, along with any recommendations of the board.

The Reformed Christian school society board represents all members of the association. However, it has special authority-responsibilities to the parents, the teachers, and the students of the school which the board operates. The board must see to it that all three interrelate properly and that each individual gets attention according to the individual's personal needs.

The authority-responsibilities of parents

The parents, as the mature members of the family, have the primary authority-responsibility to nurture the children God has given to the family. In the broader context, it is the primary authority-responsibility of parents to see to it that the board hires Christian teachers who will

---

*The use of the term *authority-responsibility* is explained in Chapter 4, *Education and the Family,* in the section on "Accountable authority-responsibility."

educate the students according to the basis article of the constitution or bylaws, and whose life is in harmony with that basis. On the other hand, the parents have the authority-responsibility to give their full support and assistance to the Christian teacher so that the continuity and cooperation between home and school may be evident to the children. Thus, this special authority-responsibility of the parents for the education of their children is a two-way street.

The boards of many Reformed Christian schools have recognized that special parent-teacher relationship. These boards have encouraged the parents and teachers to set up a parent-teacher or home-school association. Such associations are not a formal part of the school society but are auxiliary to the society and board. In these associations, parents and teachers can deal with issues which are of primary concern to the parent-teacher unity as both parents and teachers work out their peculiar task of nurturing the children in the fear of the Lord.

It is because of that interrelationship that parents and teachers are often in the best position to advise the board on matters of policy and discipline. The parent-teacher group does not have policy-making authority-responsibilities but can and often does serve as a responsible advisory body to the board.

The authority-responsibilities of teachers

Aside from the special parent-teacher relationship, the teachers have responsibilities to the board and authority-responsibilities to the students. Christian teachers have the unique authority-responsibility of teaching the child while he is in school. That teaching must be in full agreement with the fundamental principles of the school, which will include the requirement that teachers are members in good standing of an evangelical church which accepts one or more of the Reformed creedal statements listed earlier under the heading "Who can be members of a Reformed Christian school society?"

It is the authority-responsibility of the teachers in the Reformed Christian school to implement the desires and policies of the school society and its board. This is the teacher's constitutional mandate. In general terms it can be said that the board which represents the society has primary authority-responsibility to determine the content, scope and direction of the educational program of the school. The teachers, as experts in their field, have primary authority-responsibility for the methods and structure of the curriculum and instruction. Both school boards and teachers are accountable for their particular authority-responsibility to the sovereign God.

Teachers also have a very great authority-responsibility towards the students. Together with the parents and the educational ministry of the church, the teachers' *first authority-responsibility* is to lead the students to Christ so that the students, through the working of the Holy Spirit, may also come to accept Jesus as their personal Savior and Lord. Teachers spend more active time with children during the school year than do parents. For that reason teachers have a very great influence on the students, and therefore a great accountability to God, responsibility to the parents, and authority-responsibility to the students. The teachers' accountability in that first authority-responsibility is a direct result of the covenant obligation. The *second authority-responsibility* cannot be satisfied unless the first has come to fruition. (See again Chapter 1, *The Word of God and Man*, especially the section on "The salvation of man.")

The second authority-responsibility of the teachers in a

Christian school is to lead the students to respond to themselves, to others, and to creation in general so that they may serve God in whatever area of life the students may find their calling. It is impossible for the students to learn, understand, and live a life of Biblically faithful relationships without first receiving the insight which accepts Jesus Christ as Savior and Lord of His Kingdom.

These two distinct but interwoven authority-responsibilities of the Christian teachers do not come out in different subject matter and emphases in the curriculum of the earlier as compared to the later school years. Rather, it comes out in a faithfully integrated curriculum and instruction that stresses the revelation of God in the Bible *and* creation, and which attempts to show the students the proper response to the directives of God in His revelation. That twofold emphasis is inherent in every subject taught in a Reformed Christian school.

Teachers, like parents, serve as instruments of the Holy Spirit who prepares the heart to respond in the right way. That response is not limited and narrowed, as in the "altar call" approach; it is a continual response which grows as one's understanding of God's revelation and His directives for life increases. Since the teachers occupy such a vital nurturing function, they also must give evidence of the Spirit-filled life of which Galatians 5:22-6 speaks:

> But the fruit of the Spirit is love, joy, peace, patience, kindness, goodness, faithfulness, gentleness, self-control; against such there is no law. And those who belong to Christ Jesus have crucified the flesh with its passions and desires.
>
> If we live by the Spirit, let us also walk by the Spirit. Let us have no self-conceit, no provoking of one another, no envy of one another.

Christian teachers who know the gravity of their authority-responsibility through their teaching and life-style will lead the students to desire the *insight* of a Spirit-filled life of response to God. Those teachers know that the alternative is a life which responds to and serves the spirit of darkness.

Who are students in a Reformed Christian school?

The Reformed Christian school society or association is strongly committed to the concept that the home is primarily accountable for education. This means that parents have the authority-responsibility to select the school their children will attend. In making that choice, non-Christian parents are sometimes attracted to the Reformed Christian school because of a desire for discipline and/or "quality" education. Such applications for enrolment raise the question whether students from non-Christian homes should be enrolled in the Reformed Christian school.

The Reformed Christian school exists primarily to educate the children of the school society's members. According to the usual requirements for society membership, non-Christian parents cannot become members of the school society. However, in spite of that restriction, the non-Christian parent may still wish to "buy disciplines, quality, Christian education."

The primary function of the school is educational, not evangelistic. Also, the Reformed concept of education stresses the interrelationships between home, church, and school. It would seem that children from non-Christian homes lack the continuity of Biblically based nurture — which can have two results. First, such children can become totally confused because of the opposing views of life which come to expression in the home and the school. Second, it might be that the non-Christian students (especially if their enrolment becomes a sizable percentage of the student body) will cause disunity and disharmony, influencing the children of believing parents toward non-Christian attitudes. Because of these two potential problems, Reformed Christian schools may discourage or deny enrolment to the children of non-Christian parents.

It sometimes happens that non-Christian parents request the enrolment of their children in a Reformed Christian school as a result of a mission outreach of a local evangelical church. If such children are also enrolled in the educational ministry of the evangelical church, enrolment in the school may be granted as a significant auxiliary service to the mission outreach of that church. In that case the motive for — and the conditions surrounding — the application are quite different from those of non-Christian parents who only want to "buy quality education."

Believing parents who are not members in good standing of an evangelical orthodox church which accepts one or more of the creeds listed earlier and who are therefore not eligible for membership in the society may still be allowed to enroll their children in most Reformed Christian schools. Most school societies will ask such parents to read and subscribe to the basis, purpose, and educational policies of the school as a condition for their children's enrolment.

The responsibility of students

Students in a Reformed Christian school have direct responsibilities to their parents, teachers, and fellow students.

The students' responsibility to their teachers is the same as their responsibility in the home. They must understand that the teachers are performing their task at the request of — and in the place of — the parents. The parents enrol the student in the school. They pay the costs of the student's education. As in everything else, students have an obligation to their parents and are accountable to God to do the best they can in learning and responding in the classroom.

As in the case of parents and teachers, the responsibilities and relationships are a two-way street, even though the task of teachers and students differ. Teachers are accountable to God and responsible to the school society to give solid leadership and direction in helping students gain an understanding of the unity and purpose of man and the creation. With the help of the Holy Spirit, that understanding should deepen and become genuine insight. Students in the lower grades *submit* eagerly to the leadership and direction of their teachers who help them gain understanding. The Christian teachers in the lower grades begin systematically to unfold the mysteries of true knowledge based on faith in the sovereign lordship of Jesus Christ, who is the teacher's personal Savior.

As the students' understanding increases, so does their responsibility for their actions to their teachers and their accountability for their responses to God. In the higher grades, students should *submit* and *actively respond* to the leadership and direction of their teachers. That active response will be a constant feedback to the teachers, not only to evaluate the students' progress but also to guide them towards the *insight* to be bestowed on them by the Holy Spirit. Students and teachers, each in their particular task, must work at equipping the students for the battle between the Kingdom of Christ and the kingdom of satan. What is needed for that battle is the armor described in Ephesians 6:10-18:

> Finally, be strong in the Lord and in the strength of his might. Put on the whole armor of God, that you may be able to stand against the wiles of the devil. For we are not contending against flesh and blood, but against the principalities, against the powers, against the world rulers of this present darkness, against the spiritual hosts of wickedness in the heavenly places. Therefore take the whole armor of God, that you may be able to withstand in the evil

THE REFORMED CHRISTIAN SCHOOL 101

day, and having done all, to stand. Stand therefore, having girded your loins with truth, and having put on the breastplate of righteousness, and having shod your feet with the equipment of the gospel of peace; besides all these, taking the shield of faith, with which you can quench all the flaming darts of the evil one. And take the helmet of salvation, and the sword of the Spirit, which is the word of God. Pray at all times in the Spirit, with all prayer and supplication. To that end keep alert with all perseverance, making supplication for all the saints . . . .

There is also the responsibility of the students to their fellow students. Students in a school are usually referred to as the "student body." If the analogy of the body is applied, then it should become clear to the students that there are many different talents and levels of ability in any classroom. In the school situation, students must learn the meaning of the summary of the law, namely, that we are not only to love God above all but also to love our neighbors as ourselves. In the school situation, the students' neighbors are their fellow students, each with unique needs. Students must become sensitive to each other's needs and learn to help each other.

If some students have special abilities and talents, they may not use those gifts to monopolize class time or to dominate their classmates. The responsibility of such students is to serve their fellow students in the same way that Christ served. The teachers can lead these students to understand that responsibility by what Jesus said in Matthew 20:25-8:

> You know that the rulers of the Gentiles lord it over them, and their great men exercise authority over them. It shall not be so among you; but whoever would be great among you must be your servant, and whoever would be first among you must be your slave; even as the Son of man came not to be served but to serve, and to give his life as a ransom for many.

Responsibility of a Christian community

Students in the Reformed Christian school are being prepared to become members of Christ's Church so that they can serve in God's Kingdom. Christ's Church embraces all believers, and all believers are part of the covenant which God established with Abraham (Gen. 17). The promises of the covenant were for Abraham and his whole household, which included those adopted by purchase (Gen. 17:12-13). In Acts, the covenant promise is repeated immediately after the coming of the Holy Spirit at Pentecost. On that occasion Peter states:

> For the promise is to you and to your children and to all that are far off, every one whom the Lord our God calls to him (Acts 2:39).

That promise of salvation is especially strong for children from faithful Christian homes. God has shown in His Word that His Spirit works primarily by way of the family line. The ten commandments show what the result will be if the home is *not* faithful to God's covenant. In the second commandment God promises *punishment* or *blessing* right after He gives the commandment not to serve anything but Him. God says:

> You shall not make for yourself a graven image, or any likeness of anything that is in heaven above, or that is in the earth beneath, or that is in the water under the earth; you shall not bow down to them or serve them; for I the Lord your God am a jealous God, visiting the iniquity of the fathers upon the children to the third and the fourth generation of those who hate me, but showing steadfast love to thousands of those who love me and keep my commandments (Ex. 20:4-6).

In view of the eternal results of obedience or disobedience to God's law, all members of Christ's Church in the local Christian community have an authority-responsibility to *encourage* and *assist* Christian parents to obey the command of Deuteronomy 6:7 in a *conscious* and *continual* way. That commandment, though primarily given to parents, is given also to all believers in the Christian community. Since Christians *are* their brothers' keeper and since they *are* also members of the family of God, all members of Christ's Church are obliged to nurture children of believing parents with whom they directly or indirectly come in contact "in the fear of the Lord." Such nurture must be not only in words but through a Christian life-style as well, as the Bible points out:

> And these words which I command you this day shall be upon your heart; and you shall teach them diligently to your children, and shall talk of them when you sit in your house, and when you walk by the way, and when you lie down, and when you rise. And you shall bind them as a sign upon your hand, and they shall be as frontlets between your eyes. And you shall write them on the doorposts of your house and on your gates (Deut. 6:6-9).

Since Christian education is established in obedience to God's command, since punishment or blessing comes to men as a result of their response to God's command, and since Christian education contributes directly to the advancement of Christ's Kingdom, every member of the Christian community is not only obligated but should also have a holy desire to help establish and maintain Reformed Christian schools. The Christian school is an essential part of any Christian community.

The authority-responsibilities are interrelated

The distinct authority-responsibilities of boards, parents, teachers, and the members of the Christian community in general, as explained in the foregoing, do not exhaust the authority-responsibilities of the various parts of the Reformed Christian school. The faithful, Biblically-directed functioning of the Reformed Christian school requires wholesome interaction of all segments of the Christian community. All the various parts of the Reformed Christian body must fulfill their unique task in complete co-responsibility to provide unique Reformed Christian education. The best way to describe that interrelationship and interaction of the various parts of the Reformed Christian school body is found in I Corinthians 12:14-26:

> For the body does not consist of one member but of many. If the foot should say, "Because I am not a hand, I do not belong to the body," that would not make it any less a part of the body. And if the ear should say, "Because I am not an eye, I do not belong to the body," that would not make it any less a part of the body. If the whole body were an eye, where would be the hearing? If the whole body were an ear, where would be the sense of smell? But as it is, God arranged the organs in the body, each one of them, as he chose. If all were a single organ, where would the body be? As it is, there are many parts, yet one body. The eye cannot say to the hand, "I have no need of you," nor again the head to the feet, "I have no need of you." On the contrary, the parts of the body which seem to be weaker are indispensable, and those parts of the body which we think less honorable we invest with the greater honor, and our unpresentable parts are treated with greater modesty, which our more presentable parts do not require. But God has so composed the body, giving the greater honor to the inferior part, that there may be no discord in the body, but that the members may have the same care for one another. If one member suffers, all suffer together; if one member is honored, all rejoice together.

8
The International Union
of Christian Schools

The structure of the Union

Most schools in the Reformed tradition as outlined in earlier chapters are organized into an international union called the *International Union of Christian Schools*. That Union is basically a service organization for member schools and for societies not yet having schools. It operates in the United States, Canada, and even worldwide.

The headquarters of that international union or association of Christian schools is in Grand Rapids, Michigan, an area quite centrally located for the North American member schools.

Union schools are divided into twelve geographical regions called *Districts*. Eight Districts are exclusively in the United States, three are exclusively in Canada, and one covers the midwestern part of both countries. These Union Districts elect their own executive boards and carry out their own programs to serve Union schools in addition to services provided directly by Union headquarters. Some Districts are highly organized with a staff and unique District-wide services of their own; others are more loosely associated, providing very few services beyond those provided by headquarters.

Districts elect representatives to the Union Board of Directors. Each District may elect at least one member to the Union Board. When a District has 26 schools within its boundaries, it elects an additional Union Board member. Thereafter, one additional Board member is elected for every additional thirteen schools in the District, to a maximum of four Directors per District.

The Union Board of Directors governs and supervises all Union activities and programs. It meets twice a year, in March and again in August, at the time of the annual Christian School Convention.

The Union holds an annual membership meeting in conjunction with the Christian School Convention. All member schools send an official delegate to vote on issues presented to the annual meeting as detailed in the agenda. The agenda is prepared by the Union staff under the supervision of the Board of Directors and contains all reports and resolutions to be presented at the meeting. Each member school or District may present matters to the Board of Directors for inclusion on that agenda. The completed agenda is mailed to each member association well in advance of the annual meeting so that the member societies can properly instruct their delegates.

Membership requirements and obligations

A school society can become member of the Union by giving evidence in its application that its constitution substantially agrees with the basis, principles, and programs of the Union.

As a service organization, the Union does not legislate for member schools. Most of its recommendations and policies are advisory. From time to time, however, standards and policies are adopted by the membership meeting which affect relationships between member schools. In such cases the Union reserves the right to expel a member if the standards and policies are flagrantly disregarded.

The basis of the Union

The basis of the Union of Christian Schools is the Scriptures, Old Testament and New, the infallible Word of God, as explicated in Reformed creedal standards. On this basis the Union affirms the following principles for Christian education:

The Bible. That God by His Holy Word reveals Himself; renews man's understanding of God, of man himself, of his fellowman, and of the world; directs man in all his relationships and activities; and therefore guides His people also in the education of their children.

Creation. That in their education children must come to learn that the world, and man's calling in it, can rightly be understood only in their relation to the Triune God who by His creation, restoration, and governance directs all things to the coming of His kingdom and the glorification of His name.

Sin. That because man's sin, which brought upon all mankind the curse of God, alienates him from his Creator, his neighbor, and the world; distorts his view of the true meaning and purpose of life; and misdirects human culture; man's sin also corrupts the education of children.

Jesus Christ. That through our Savior, Jesus Christ, there is renewal of our educational enterprise because He is the Redeemer of, and the Light and the Way for, our human life in all its range and variety. Only through Him and the work of His Spirit are we guided in the truth and recommitted to our original calling.

Schools. That the purpose of Christian schools is to educate children for a life of obedience to their calling in this world as image-bearers of God; that this calling is to know God's Word and His creation, to consecrate the whole of human life to God, to love their fellowman, and to be stewards in their God-given cultural task.

Parents. That the primary responsibility for education rests upon parents to whom children are entrusted by God, and that Christian parents should accept this obligation in view of the covenantal relationship which God established with believers and their children. They should seek to discharge this obligation through school associations and school boards which engage the services of Christian teachers in Christian schools.

Teachers. That Christian teachers, both in obedience to God and in cooperation with parents, have a unique pedagogical responsibility while educating the child in school.

Pupils. That Christian schools must take into account the variety of abilities, needs, and responsibilities of young persons; that the endowments and calling of young persons as God's image-bearers and their defects and inadequacies as sinners require that such learning goals and such curricula will be selected as will best prepare them to live as obedient Christians; and that only with constant attention to such pedagogical concerns will education be truly Christian.

Community. That because God's covenant embraces not only parents and their children but also the whole Christian community to which they belong, and because Christian education contributes directly to the advancement of God's kingdom, it is the obligation not only of the parents but also of their Christian community to establish and maintain Christian schools, to pray for, work for, and give generously to their support.

Educational Freedom. That Christian schools, organized and administered in accordance with legitimate standards and provisions for day schools, should be fully recognized in society as free to function according to their principles.

Services of the Union

The Union provides a number of services to its member school societies — assistance in establishing new schools; administration of pension and insurance plans; inspection and evaluation of member schools; development and publication of curriculum materials; activities and materials that affect school and government relations; promotional and other materials that affect the school and its public relations.

In its curriculum development and publishing responsibilities, the Union is financially assisted by two independent but associated Christian Education Foundations, namely, the Christian School Educational Foundation in the United States and the Canadian Christian Education Foundation Inc. in Canada. While more information about the Union, the two foundations, and the services available to member school societies may be obtained directly from the Union, the following description will give an idea of some of those services.

Establishing Schools. The Union has a planning kit that will help any group of Christian parents and friends establish and operate a Christian school. *A Board Member's Handbook* has also been developed and is an invaluable guide for the establishment and operation of a Christian school society and school.

Administering Pension and Insurance Plans. Member schools in the United States operate the *Christian School Pension Plan and Trust Fund* and the *Group Insurance Plan and Trust Fund.* These plans and funds are operated by a Board of Trustees with equal school society and teacher representation. Independent of, but parallel to, the U.S. plans and funds, are the *Canadian Christian School Pension Plan and Trust Fund* and the *Canadian Group Insurance Plan and Trust Fund.* Each of these plans and funds exists to provide insurance, health, dental, and retirement benefits to eligible staff members of the participating member schools. The Union provides the administrative services for these plans and funds.

Inspection and Evaluation of Member Schools. The Union offers inspection and evaluation services to any member school that requests them. The services are normally offered on a rotating basis to specific geographic areas. It is important for a school society to be aware of how the overall facilities, programs, curriculum, and staff of its school compares with other Christian schools. These evaluations can help bring further development priorities into focus.

Developing and Publishing Curriculum. It is probably obvious that most of the time, effort and money of the Union is spent in developing Christian curriculum materials. From the presentations and discussions in this book, it is clear that Reformed Christian schools cannot use most of the curriculum materials that are used in other school systems, whether public or private. Much has been done in the Christian curriculum area, and much more needs to be done. Curriculum development is never finished; it is an ongoing task. The curriculum is developed to show how every subject area belongs to, and can only be understood within, the total framework God provided in the Bible and creation. The materials are written by qualified teachers; tested and evaluated in pilot schools; revised on the basis of the pilot schools' findings and recommendations; tested again; and finally published for general use. (A free catalogue of Union materials will be sent on request to anyone interested.)

School and Government Relations. There are a number of areas in which state and provincial governments have a legitimate effect on the operation of alternate and independent schools. These areas usually are that:

 (1) Students must have reached a certain age before they are allowed to leave school.

 (2) There must be a minimum number of school days during the year.

 (3) Minimum standards of program and curriculum must be met.

 (4) Buildings must meet health and safety standards.

 (5) Teachers must have basic competence or qualifications.

Other regulations and guidelines which are obligatory to public schools are usually advisory for alternate and independent schools. It is important that good relations be maintained with all levels of government involved with education, so that the Christian schools retain a maximum amount of self-governance. The Union operates a department to look after these interests.

School and Public Relations. This is the Union department which deals with internal (inter-school) and external promotion and public relations. It is primarily responsible for the Union's official publication—*Christian Home and School* magazine. This department also produces promotional materials such as Christian Education Week materials, audio-visual presentations, promotional handbooks, bulletin covers and inserts, and pamphlets. These materials are available for purchase by school societies at a nominal cost.

The Christian education foundations in Canada and the United States are two independent foundations which support the educational programs of the Union. More specifically, they help underwrite the publication of Christian textbooks and teacher aids for use in Christian schools. Although they are not directly responsible to the Union or its member schools, the Union receives a voluntary accounting from each foundation and has its own representatives on their boards. The Union also endorses both foundations. The two foundations raise thousands of dollars annually for the much needed development and publication of Christian curricula from a Reformed viewpoint on life and the world. Christians who read these pages and who desire to see children educated from the point of view explained in this book might consider a donation to either one of these foundations. The addresses are:

Christian School Educational Foundation
865 - 28th Street SE
Grand Rapids, Michigan, 49508

Canadian Christian Education Foundation Inc.
2389 St. Francis Drive
Burlington, Ontario, L7P 1V3

All those who donate to the foundation in their country of residence will receive a receipt for tax deduction purposes.

This is only a brief description of some of the Union services. Anyone interested in more information can write directly to the Union at 865 - 28th Street SE, Grand Rapids, Michigan, 49508.

Index

Index